CENTRAL 2NDFLOOR
0202300242411
811 A887.2
Atwood, Marg   P9-CTB-472
Two-headed poems /

KALAMAZOO PUBLIC LIBRARY

MAY   1981

DEMCO

BY MARGARET ATWOOD

Poetry
THE CIRCLE GAME
THE ANIMALS IN THAT COUNTRY
THE JOURNALS OF SUSANNA MOODIE
PROCEDURES FOR UNDERGROUND
POWER POLITICS
YOU ARE HAPPY
SELECTED POEMS
TWO-HEADED POEMS

Fiction
THE EDIBLE WOMAN
SURFACING
LADY ORACLE
DANCING GIRLS
LIFE BEFORE MAN

Criticism
SURVIVAL:
  A THEMATIC GUIDE TO CANADIAN LITERATURE

FOR J. AND G.

81 05266

811
A887.2

MY WARMEST THANKS TO DENNIS LEE, AS USUAL.

COPYRIGHT © 1978 BY MARGARET ATWOOD.
ALL RIGHTS RESERVED
INCLUDING THE RIGHT OF REPRODUCTION
IN WHOLE OR IN PART IN ANY FORM.
A TOUCHSTONE BOOK
PUBLISHED BY SIMON AND SCHUSTER,
A DIVISION OF GULF & WESTERN CORPORATION.
SIMON & SCHUSTER BUILDING,
ROCKEFELLER CENTER,
1230 AVENUE OF THE AMERICAS,
NEW YORK, NEW YORK 10020.
SIMON AND SCHUSTER AND COLOPHON ARE TRADEMARKS OF
    SIMON & SCHUSTER.
TOUCHSTONE AND COLOPHON ARE TRADEMARKS OF
    SIMON & SCHUSTER
DESIGNED BY EVE METZ

MANUFACTURED IN THE UNITED STATES OF AMERICA

PUBLISHED IN CANADA BY OXFORD UNIVERSITY PRESS IN 1978.
10 9 8 7 6 5 4 3 2 1
10 9 8 7 6 5 4 3 2 1   Pbk.
LIBRARY OF CONGRESS CATALOGING IN PUBLICATION DATA
ATWOOD, MARGARET ELEANOR, DATE.
    TWO-HEADED POEMS.
    (A TOUCHSTONE BOOK)
    I. TITLE.
PR9199.3.A8T85   1980   811'.54   80-19276
ISBN 0-671-25370-0
ISBN 0-671-25373-5 Pbk.

Some of these poems have appeared in the following magazines and anthologies:

Exile, Canadian Forum, Waves, Capilano Review, This Magazine, Acta Victoriana, 52 Pickups, Divided We Stand (Canada)

(Continued on page 113)

TWO-HEADED POEMS

Margaret Atwood

A TOUCHSTONE BOOK
PUBLISHED BY SIMON AND SCHUSTER
NEW YORK

KALAMAZOO PUBLIC LIBRARY

CONTENTS

•

BURNED SPACE

What comes in after a burn?
You could say nothing,

but there are flowers like dampened embers
that burst in cool white smoke

and after that, blue lights
among the leaves

that grow at the bases
of these blackened monoliths.

Before the burn, this was a forest.
Now it is something else:

a burn twists the green
eternal into singed gray

history: these discarded
stag-heads and small charred bones.

In a burn you kneel among the
reddish flowers and glowing seeds,

you give thanks as after a disaster
you were not part of,

though any burn
might have been your skin:

despite these liquid petals
against smoked rock, after a burn

your hands are never the same.

FORETELLING THE FUTURE

It doesn't matter how it is done,
these hints, these whispers:

whether it is some god
blowing through your head
as through a round bone
flute, or bright
stones fallen on the sand

or a charlatan, stringing you
a line with bird gut,

or smoke, or the taut hair
of a dead girl singing.

It doesn't matter what is said

but you can feel
those crystal hands, stroking
the air around your body
till the air glows white

and you are like the moon
seen from the earth, oval and gentle
and filled with light.

The moon seen from the moon
is a different thing.

A PAPER BAG

I make my head, as I used to,
out of a paper bag,
pull it down to the collarbone,

draw eyes around my eyes,
with purple and green
spikes to show surprise,
a thumb-shaped nose,

a mouth around my mouth
penciled by touch, then colored in
flat red.

With this new head, the body now
stretched like a stocking and exhausted could
dance again; if I made a
tongue I could sing.

An old sheet and it's Halloween;
but why is it worse or more

frightening, this pinface
head of square hair and no chin?

Like an idiot, it has no past
and is always entering the future
through its slots of eyes, purblind
and groping with its thick smile,
a tentacle of perpetual joy.

Paper head, I prefer you
because of your emptiness;
from within you any
word could still be said.

With you I could have
more than one skin,
a blank interior, a repertoire
of untold stories,
a fresh beginning.

THE WOMAN WHO
COULD NOT LIVE
WITH HER FAULTY HEART

I do not mean the symbol
of love, a candy shape
to decorate cakes with,
the heart that is supposed
to belong or break;

I mean this lump of muscle
that contracts like a flayed biceps,
purple-blue, with its skin of suet,
its skin of gristle, this isolate,
this caved hermit, unshelled
turtle, this one lungful of blood,
no happy plateful.

All hearts float in their own
deep oceans of no light,
wetblack and glimmering,
their four mouths gulping like fish.
Hearts are said to pound:
this is to be expected, the heart's
regular struggle against being drowned.

But most hearts say, I want, I want,
I want, I want. My heart
is more duplicitous,
though no twin as I once thought.
It says, I want, I don't want, I
want, and then a pause.
It forces me to listen,

and at night it is the infra-red
third eye that remains open
while the other two are sleeping
but refuses to say what it has seen.

It is a constant pestering
in my ears, a caught moth, limping drum,
a child's fist beating
itself against the bedsprings:
I want, I don't want.
How can one live with such a heart?

Long ago I gave up singing
to it, it will never be satisfied or lulled.
One night I will say to it:
Heart, be still,
and it will.

FIVE POEMS FOR DOLLS

i

Behind glass in Mexico
this clay doll draws
its lips back in a snarl;
despite its beautiful dusty shawl,
it wishes to be dangerous.

ii

See how the dolls resent us,
with their bulging foreheads
and minimal chins, their flat bodies
never allowed to bulb and swell,
their faces of little thugs.

This is not a smile,
this glossy mouth, two stunted teeth;
the dolls gaze at us
with the filmed eyes of killers.

iii

There have always been dolls
as long as there have been people.
In the trash heaps and abandoned temples
the dolls pile up;
the sea is filling with them.

What causes them?
Or are they gods, causeless,
something to talk to
when you have to talk,
something to throw against the wall?

A doll is a witness
who cannot die,
with a doll you are never alone.

On the long journey under the earth,
in the boat with two prows,
there were always dolls.

iv

Or did we make them
because we needed to love someone
and could not love each other?

It was love, after all,
that rubbed the skins from their gray cheeks,
crippled their fingers,
snarled their hair, brown or dull gold.
Hate would merely have smashed them.

You change, but the doll
I made of you lives on,
a white body leaning
in a sunlit window, the features
wearing away with time,
frozen in the gaunt pose
of a single day,
holding in its plaster hand
your doll of me.

V

Or: all dolls come
from the land of the unborn,
the almost-born; each
doll is a future
dead at the roots, ·
a voice heard only
on breathless nights,
a desolate white memento.

Or: these are the lost children,
those who have died or thickened
to full growth and gone away.

The dolls are their souls or cast skins
which line the shelves of our bedrooms
and museums, disguised as outmoded toys,
images of our sorrow,
shedding around themselves
five inches of limbo.

TWO MILES AWAY

Two miles away, the humid weekend
jerks in thin lights along the highway,
bumper to bumper, groups
and separates at the corner store,
which could be anywhere.

But this is the hinterland: layer
of grass, layer of lukewarm dirt, layer of stones,
layer of winter.

Oblongs of earth, edged with fences;
in the middle of each, two sleepers.

Night rises from their bodies
and spreads over the hills,
musty, smelling of thunder;
the air around their heads
thickens with ancestors.

This is the land of hope
fulfilled, this is a desert;
like deserts it is nocturnal
and planted with bones.

Outside this house, the hammock
weaves one tree to another.
For once there is no wind.
Sandbox in moonlight, the glimmer
of shadowy toys, the green shovel,
the cracked white pail, the red star.

In the turned furrows, around our bed,
wild carrots, pinkish-mauve and stealthy,
creep over the rug, the cleared space,
an invasion of savage flowers
reclaiming their lost territory.

Is this where I want to be,
is this who I want to be with,

half of a pair,
half of a custom,
nose against neck, knee thrown
over the soft groin,

part of this ancient habit,
part of this net, this comfort,
this redblack night,
humility of the sleeping body,
web of blood.

TODAY

•

Today the lawn holds
my daughter like a hostage
where she walks, not as high
as the wrecked picnic table,
through the scant grass, burdock leaves
made ragged by the mower,
tripping, stopping
to pick up and put down.

(Watch the slope, hard clay with bladed
stones, posing
innocuous as daisies:
it leads down to the pond,
where the ducks beckon, eleven
of them, they are saying:
        feathers.   feathers.)

The lure of eleven birds
on water, the glitter
and true shine, how can I tell her
that white, that bluegreen gold
is treachery?

Each of these rescues
costs me something,
a loss, a dulling
of this bluegold eye.

Later she will learn
about edges. Or better, find
by luck or a longer journey
the shadow of that liquid
gold place, which can be
so single and clear for her
only now, when it means danger
only to me.

NOTHING NEW HERE

Nothing new here; just rain
in the afternoon, anger, two minutes of hail
that punched holes in the broad leaves;
then moist sun.

In the clearing air
we crouch in the garden, reconciled
for the moment, pulling out weeds.
Ragweed, pigweed, milkweed,
we know the names by now.
This is the fifth year.

Nothing stays free, though on what ought
to be the lawn, thistles blossom, their flowers
as purple as if I'd bought them;
around the edges of our cage,
outside the wire, there's the dying
rose hedge the mice ate.

What defeats us, as always, is
the repetition: weather
we can't help, habits we don't break.
The frogs, with their dud guitar-
string throats, every spring, release
their songs of love, while slugs breed
in the rain under the hay

we use for barricades;
milkweed and pigweed, the purslane
spreading its fleshy
starfish at our feet,
grabbing for space.

We know the names by now;
will that make anything better?
Our love is clumsier
each year, words knot
and harden, grow sideways, devious as grass.

Admit it,
this is what we have made,
this ragged place, an order
gone to seed, the battered plants
slump in the tangled rows,
their stems and damp rope sagging.
Our blunted fingers,
our mouths taste
of the same earth, bitter and deep.
(Though this is also what we have
in common; this broken
garden, measure
of our neglect and failure, still
gives what we eat.)

DAYBOOKS I

.

1

This is the somewhere
we were always trying to get:
landscape
reduced to the basics:
rolling mills, rocks, running
water, burdocks, trees living and dead,
the gambler's potato acres
brown money stuck in rows.
On this high ground, one late
frost or month of sun
finishes him.

No rain for weeks now, dust
twists across the fields,
the thigh-high clover
with its blossoms of white spittle
is sucked back into the ground.

2

Midnight: my house rests
on arrowheads and toebones,
scraps of raw fur, a cellar
scooped from the trashgrounds
of whatever ancestors once also
passed through time here,
shedding themselves piecemeal
in their long trek to sunset.

Things we are leaving:
bushel baskets and broken glass,
a knitted hand squashed flat,
potatoes that sprout and rot,
a rubber foot.

In this leaking boat I sail downhill
from one day to the next.

3

Someone came here, blunted
several good plowshares,
cursed the groundhogs and their
ankle-breaking burrows,
hauled rocks until he died,
bursting a vein
out of sight of the house.
He had no sons, or if he did
they went elsewhere.

Stonepile in the back field,
overgrown by lichens, purple
nightshade, spindly raspberry,
the frame and springs of a sleigh.

We inherited this cairn
he and some glacier raised
to no memory in particular.

In one week we unbuild him,
pillage his limestone, shale,
red granite, delicate fossils.

This is the rock garden.
In it, the stones
too are flowers.

The rocks will stay
where they are put, for the time
being.

4

Eleven and no moon, the power
dead again, full weight
of August presses against my ears
with its chirps and dry whispers.

Downstairs, my daughter sleeps
in her jungle of pastel animals
with their milky noses and missing eyes;
green leaves are rising around her cage,
rubbery and huge, where she hunts and snuffles
on all fours through the hours;
she has eaten the eyes of the lion
and is the lion.

I stand in the upstairs hall
groping for stairwell; cat feet drip
through the darkness, threading the labyrinth
toward the sound of water.

What is there to dread, where
are the candles? My heart jumps
in the end of my left thumb,
small as a grape.

There is nothing to do but try
for courage, one stair and then
the next and hope
for vision, fearing

I have gone blind
but don't yet know it.

(I write this later, waiting
for the real thing.)

5

LETTERS

Almost winter, and in the gravel drive-
way under the stripped trees

a stack of dried voices clamoring
for replies. What can I tell you? That I

no longer live here?

I do not know
the manner of your deaths, daily
or final, blood
will not flow in the fossil
heart at my command, I can't
put the life back into those
lives, those lies. I know

where I live and it is not
in this box. If you need
the elixir of love
from me, you need
more than anyone can give.

As for the questions: How
am I? Can I, could I?
I can't, I never could;
I am / not.

6

AFTER JAYNES

The old queen's head cut off
at the neck, then skinned & emptied,
boiled, coated with plaster,
cheeks and lips dyed red,
bright stones in the eyes

  After this transformation
  she can sing,
  can tell us what we think
  we need to hear

  This is "poetry," this song
  of the wind across teeth,
  this message from the flayed tongue
  to the flayed ear.

7

November, the empty month; we try
to fill it with the smells
of cooking earth: baked roots, the comfort
of windfall pears, potatoes
floury and round, onions
& vinegar simmer
on the black stove, & the air
fogs with sugar; the risen bread says
this is where
we live,
      brave statement.

At night we make a fire
not for the warmth so much as for
the light
      & the old pumpkin
      lantern, our emblem,
      burns and shrivels, falling
      in upon itself, a gaunt
      sun, end
      of this year.

FIVE POEMS FOR GRANDMOTHERS

i

In the house on the cliff
by the ocean, there is still a shell
bigger and lighter than your head, though now
you can hardly lift it.

It was once filled with whispers;
it was once a horn
you could blow like a shaman
conjuring the year,
and your children would come running.

You've forgotten you did that,
you've forgotten the names of the children
who in any case no longer run,
and the ocean has retreated,
leaving a difficult beach of gray stones
you are afraid to walk on.

The shell is now a cave
which opens for you alone.
It is still filled with whispers
which escape into the room,
even though you turn it mouth down.

This is your house, this is the picture
of your misty husband, these are your children, webbed
and doubled. This is the shell,

which is hard, which is still there,
solid under the hand, which mourns, which offers
itself, a narrow journey
along its hallways of cold pearl
down the cliff into the sea.

ii

It is not the things themselves
that are lost, but their use and handling.

The ladder first; the beach;
the storm windows, the carpets;

The dishes, washed daily
for so many years the pattern
has faded; the floor, the stairs, your own
arms and feet whose work
you thought defined you;

The hairbrush, the oil stove
with its many failures,
the apple tree and the barrels
in the cellar for the apples,
the flesh of apples; the judging
of the flesh, the recipes
in tiny brownish writing
with the names of those who passed them
from hand to hand: Gladys,
Lorna, Winnie, Jean.

If you could only have them back
or remember who they were.

iii

How little I know
about you finally:

The time you stood
in the nineteenth century
on Yonge Street, a thousand
miles from home, with a brown purse
and a man stole it.

Six children, five who lived.
She never said anything
about those births and the one death;
her mouth closed on a pain
that could neither be told nor ignored.

She used to have such a sense of fun.
Now girls, she would say
when we would tease her.
Her anger though, why
that would curl your hair,
though she never swore.
The worst thing she could say was:
Don't be foolish.

At eighty she had two teeth pulled out
and walked the four miles home
in the noon sun, placing her feet
in her own hunched shadow.

The bibbed print aprons, the shock
of the red lace dress, the pin
I found at six in your second drawer,

made of white beads, the shape of a star.
What did we ever talk about
but food, health and the weather?

Sons branch out, but
one woman leads to another.
Finally I know you
through your daughters,
my mother, her sisters,
and through myself:

Is this you, this edgy joke
I make, are these your long fingers,
your hair of an untidy bird,
is this your outraged
eye, this grip
that will not give up?

iv

Some kind of ritual
for your dwindling,
some kind of dragon, small,
benign and wooden
with two mouths to catch your soul
because it is wandering
like a lost child, lift it back safely.

But we have nothing; we say,
How is she?
Not so good, we answer,
though some days she's fine.

On other days you walk through
the door of the room in the house
where you've lived for seventy years
and find yourself in a hallway
you know you have never seen before.

Midnight, they found her
opening and closing the door
of the refrigerator:
vistas of day-old vegetables, the used bone
of an animal, and beyond that
the white ice road that leads north.

They said, Mother,
what are you doing here?

Nothing is finished
or put away, she said.
I don't know where I am.

Against the disappearance
of outlines, against
the disappearance of sounds,
against the blurring of the ears
and eyes, against the small fears
of the very old, the fear
of mumbling, the fear of dying,
the fear of falling downstairs,
I make this charm
from nothing but paper; which is good
for exactly nothing.

v

Goodbye, mother
of my mother, old bone
tunnel through which I came.

You are sinking down into
your own veins, fingers
folding back into the hand,

day by day a slow retreat
behind the disk of your face
which is hard and netted like an ancient plate.

You will flicker in these words
and in the words of others
for a while and then go out.

Even if I send them,
you will never get these letters.
Even if I see you again,

I will never see you again.

THE MAN WITH A HOLE
IN HIS THROAT

The black hole in his throat
is the same as the black
holes in space.

He knows it only as
a quicksand of skin
above his collarbone,
an absence, a crater
at the base of his skull
into which, sooner
or later, everything falls:

His bed and the women
undulating within it,
his children, the squeezed bulb
of his heart, his shoes
and mended socks, which offer
the damp woolen comforts
of the mundane; even his laughter
which in its time bounced glasses
on the table: they are all
victims of that gradual swallow.

The hole in his throat
is hard to understand,
has never appeared, is not a wound;
to speak of filling it
or sealing it would be meaningless.
It is a personal
quirk, like a stammer
or a deformed foot,
and as relentless.

Nothing ever comes out of it,
he thinks, though sometimes words
emerge from it like oracles
or dead rabbits, and those
sitting at dinner sometimes
grow indistinct, tainted
with its darkness: have they been there?

The black hole in his throat
erodes him: around its edges
his flesh melts and vanishes.

To try to close it though
would be fatal: he needs his neck,
it keeps his head joined to that body
which night by night eludes him
like a horizon; which he still trusts.

In any case, the hole
in his throat is his: although
he does not own it, he
is its location,
he has been chosen.

He never speaks of it, he wears
high collars, his throat
holds this one secret well.

What could he say of it, this thumbnail
of nothing, this heavy cave
in himself, this numb spiral,
this miraculous pool
through which, when he looks in the mirror,
he can see the farthest stars?

NOTE FROM AN
ITALIAN POSTCARD FACTORY

Why prowl the world, hungry
and albino, with your
face of a blotter, your eyes on stalks
jerking this way and that,
rubbing yourself against
these alien landscapes, on the sniff
for the real thing?

You know you will never find it:
the muted trees shaped like umbrellas
or reversed turnips or brooms, the mountains
that were promised you recede
as you approach,
taking their unassailable
blue, leaving a space
devoid of anything but the air
in elevators.

A clean toilet is a metaphysical
assumption, your quest for which
has spoiled the view;
but you also want demons
that are still believed in.

We on the other hand
can give you the genuine item
without the pain:
no gut cramps, no swollen ankles,
no men thrusting their fingerless hands
through taxi windows.

We sell pure yodels,
camel drivers with no buses
in the background, tamed bangles
wrist to elbow on women
who don't mind,
                    the essence of wherever
you like
            and those mountains, those brief blue
mountains can be yours
as much as they are anyone's,
forever, untouched
by anything but the clouds.

FOOTNOTE TO THE
AMNESTY REPORT ON TORTURE

The torture chamber is not like anything
you would have expected.
No opera set or sexy chains and
leather-goods from the glossy
porno magazines, no thirties horror
dungeon with gauzy cobwebs; nor is it
the bare cold-lighted
chrome space of the future
we think we fear.
More like one of the seedier
British Railways stations, with scratched green
walls and spilled tea,
crumpled papers, and a stooped man
who is always cleaning the floor.

It stinks, though; like a hospital,
of antiseptics and sickness,
and, on some days, blood
which smells the same anywhere,
here or at the butcher's.

The man who works here
is losing his sense of smell.
He's glad to have this job, because
there are few others.
He isn't a torturer, he only
cleans the floor:
every morning the same vomit,

the same shed teeth, the same
piss and liquid shit, the same panic.

Some have courage, others
don't; those who do what he thinks of
as the real work, and who are
bored, since minor bureaucrats
are always bored, tell them
it doesn't matter, who
will ever know they were brave, they might
as well talk now
and get it over.

Some have nothing to say, which also
doesn't matter. Their
warped bodies too, with the torn
fingers and ragged tongues, are thrown
over the spiked iron fence onto
the Consul's lawn, along with
the bodies of the children
burned to make their mothers talk.

The man who cleans the floors
is glad it isn't him.
It will be if he ever says
what he knows. He works long hours,
submits to the searches, eats
a meal he brings from home, which tastes
of old blood and the sawdust
he cleans the floor with. His wife
is pleased he brings her money
for the food, has been told
not to ask questions.

As he sweeps, he tries
not to listen; he tries
to make himself into a wall,
a thick wall, a wall
soft and without echoes. He thinks
of nothing but the walk back
to his hot shed of a house,
of the door
opening and his children
with their unmarked skin and flawless eyes
running to meet him.

He is afraid of
what he might do
if he were told to,
he is afraid of the door,

he is afraid, not
of the door but of the door
opening; sometimes, no matter
how hard he tries,
his children are not there.

MARRYING THE HANGMAN

.

She has been condemned to death by hanging. A man may escape this death by becoming the hangman, a woman by marrying the hangman. But at the present time there is no hangman; thus there is no escape. There is only a death, indefinitely postponed. This is not fantasy, it is history.

*

To live in prison is to live without mirrors. To live without mirrors is to live without the self. She is living selflessly, she finds a hole in the stone wall and on the other side of the wall, a voice. The voice comes through darkness and has no face. This voice becomes her mirror.

*

In order to avoid her death, her particular death, with wrung neck and swollen tongue, she must marry the hangman. But there is no hangman, first she must create him, she must persuade this man at the end of the voice, this voice she has never seen and which has never seen her, this darkness, she must persuade him to renounce his face, exchange it for the impersonal mask of death, of official death which has eyes but no mouth, this mask of a dark leper. She must transform his hands so they will be willing to twist the rope around throats that have been singled out as hers was, throats other than hers. She must marry the hangman or no one, but that is not so bad. Who else is there to marry?

*

You wonder about her crime. She was condemned
to death for stealing clothes from her employer, from
the wife of her employer. She wished to make herself
more beautiful. This desire in servants was not legal.

*

She uses her voice like a hand, her voice reaches
through the wall, stroking and touching. What could
she possibly have said that would have convinced him?
He was not condemned to death, freedom awaited
him. What was the temptation, the one that worked?
Perhaps he wanted to live with a woman whose life
he had saved, who had seen down into the earth but
had nevertheless followed him back up to life. It was
his only chance to be a hero, to one person at least,
for if he became the hangman the others would
despise him. He was in prison for wounding another
man, on one finger of the right hand, with a sword.
This too is history.

*

My friends, who are both women, tell me their stories,
which cannot be believed and which are true. They
are horror stories and they have not happened to me,
they have not yet happened to me, they have
happened to me but we are detached, we watch our
unbelief with horror. Such things cannot happen to
us, it is afternoon and these things do not happen in
the afternoon. The trouble was, she said, I didn't
have time to put my glasses on and without them I'm
blind as a bat, I couldn't even see who it was. These

things happen and we sit at a table and tell stories
about them so we can finally believe. This is not
fantasy, it is history, there is more than one hangman
and because of this some of them are unemployed.

*

He said: the end of walls, the end of ropes, the opening
of doors, a field, the wind, a house, the sun, a table,
an apple.

She said: nipple, arms, lips, wine, belly, hair, bread,
thighs, eyes, eyes.

They both kept their promises.

*

The hangman is not such a bad fellow. Afterwards he
goes to the refrigerator and cleans up the leftovers,
though he does not wipe up what he accidentally
spills. He wants only the simple things: a chair,
someone to pull off his shoes, someone to watch him
while he talks, with admiration and fear, gratitude if
possible, someone in whom to plunge himself for rest
and renewal. These things can best be had by marrying
a woman who has been condemned to death by other
men for wishing to be beautiful. There is a wide
choice.

*

Everyone said he was a fool.
Everyone said she was a clever woman.
They used the word *ensnare*.

*

What did they say the first time they were alone
together in the same room? What did he say when
she had removed her veil and he could see that she
was not a voice but a body and therefore finite?
What did she say when she discovered that she had
left one locked room for another? They talked of
love, naturally, though that did not keep them
busy forever.

*

The fact is there are no stories I can tell my friends
that will make them feel better. History cannot be
erased, although we can soothe ourselves by
speculating about it. At that time there were no
female hangmen. Perhaps there have never been any,
and thus no man could save his life by marriage.
Though a woman could, according to the law.

*

He said: foot, boot, order, city, fist, roads, time,
knife.

She said: water, night, willow, rope hair, earth belly,
cave, meat, shroud, open, blood.

They both kept their promises.

FOUR SMALL ELEGIES

•

(1838, 1977)

i

BEAUHARNOIS

The bronze clock brought
with such care over the sea,
which ticked like the fat slow heart
of a cedar, of a grandmother,
melted and its hundred years
of time ran over the ice and froze there.

We are fixed by this frozen clock
at the edge of the winter forest.
Ten below zero.
Shouts in a foreign language
come down blue snow.

The women in their thin nightgowns
disappear wordlessly among the trees.
Here and there a shape,
a limp cloth bundle, a child
who could not keep up
lies sprawled face down in a drift
near the trampled clearing.

No one could give them clothes or shelter,
these were the orders.

We didn't hurt them, the man said,
we didn't touch them.

ii

BEAUHARNOIS, GLENGARRY

Those whose houses were burned
burned houses. What else ever happens
once you start?

           While the roofs plunged
into the root-filled cellars,
they chased ducks, chickens, anything
they could catch, clubbed their heads
on rock, spitted them, singed off the feathers
in fires of blazing fences,
ate them in handfuls, charred
and bloody.

           Sitting in the snow
in those mended plaids, rubbing their numb feet,
eating soot, still hungry,
they watched the houses die like
sunsets, like their own
houses. Again

those who gave the orders
were already somewhere else,
of course on horseback.

iii

BEAUHARNOIS

Is the man here, they said,
where is he?

        She didn't know, though
she called to him as they dragged her
out of the stone house by both arms
and fired the bedding.

He was gone somewhere with the other men,
he was not hanged, he came back later,
they lived in a borrowed shack,

A language is not words only,
it is the stories
that are told in it,
the stories that are never told.

He pumped himself for years
after that into her body
which had no feet
since that night, which had no fingers.
His hatred of the words
that had been done became children.

They did the best they could:
she fed them, he told them
one story only.

iv

DUFFERIN, SIMCOE, GREY

This year we are making
nothing but elegies.
Do what you are good at,
our parents always told us,
make what you know.

This is what we are making,
these songs for the dying.
You have to celebrate something.
The nets rot, the boats rot, the farms
revert to thistle, foreigners
and summer people admire the weeds
and the piles of stones dredged from the fields
by men whose teeth were gone by thirty

But the elegies are new and yellow,
they are not even made, they grow,
they come out everywhere,
in swamps, at the edges of puddles,
all over the acres
of parked cars, they are mournful
but sweet, like flowered hats
in attics we never knew we had.

We gather them, keep them in vases,
water them while our houses wither.

THE RIGHT HAND FIGHTS THE LEFT

Why should there be a war?
Once there was none.

The left hand sang the rituals,
the right hand answered.

Now, the right hand dips down
into the chemicals of its own blood
and comes up metal.

It arranges the nouns it has killed
in plaza windows,
it is odorless and dry,
it squeezes and apple plasma
drips from its fist.
It oils itself and makes lists
of its enemies, it swivels
on the wrist like a spy, a radar,
a tentacled silver eye.

The left hand, you will observe,
is soft and smaller.

It sleeps during the day
when the right hand is marching,
but that voice you heard at sunset
was the left hand calling:

Arise, O fingers
of the left hand, and outside, in a tangle
of liquid roots and the quick sprawl
of tendrils over the earth,
the forces of the left hand wake
to savage life.

An owl strikes, and mouseblood becomes owl
blood, each fur stomach
extrudes a mouth, snails
rasp against leaves, in the hearts
of purple flowers moth-
eggs multiply, the feral darkness
flickers with cactus teeth.

The right hand turns
in its sleep, moans
like a train, like a wrong turn, like a chain.

In this furious chase,
the war of the body against itself,
there is no winner, only joy
and no joy.

Dawn comes, and the right hand blasts
another tree from its burrow.

The right hand holds the knife,
the left hand dances.

TWO-HEADED POEMS

•

"Joined Head to Head, and still alive"
Advertisement for Siamese Twins,
Canadian National Exhibition, c. 1954.

The heads speak sometimes singly, sometimes
together, sometimes alternately within a poem.
Like all Siamese twins, they dream of separation.

i

Well, we felt
we were almost getting somewhere
though how that place would differ
from where we've always been, we
couldn't tell you

and then this happened,
this joke or major quake, a rift
in the earth, now everything
in the place is falling south
into the dark pit left by Cincinnati
after it crumbled.

This rubble is the future,
pieces of bureaucrats, used
bumper stickers, public names
returnable as bottles.
Our fragments made us.

What will happen to the children,
not to mention the words
we've been stockpiling for ten years now,
defining them, freezing them, storing
them in the cellar.
Anyone asked us who we were, we said
just look down there.

So much for the family business.
It was too small anyway
to be, as they say, viable.

But we weren't expecting this,
the death of shoes, fingers
dissolving from our hands,
atrophy of the tongue,
the empty mirror,
the sudden change
from ice to thin air.

ii

Those south of us are lavish
with their syllables. They scatter, we
hoard. Birds
eat their words, we eat
each other's, words, hearts, what's
the difference? In hock

up to our eyebrows, we're still
polite, god knows, to the tourists.
We make tea properly and hold the knife
the right way.

Sneering is good for you
when someone else has cornered
the tree market.

Who was it told us
so indelibly,
those who take risks
have accidents?

III

We think of you as one
big happy family, sitting around
an old pine table, trading
in-jokes, hospitable to strangers
who come from far enough away.

As for us, we're the neighbors,
we're the folks whose taste
in fences and pink iron lawn flamingoes
you don't admire.

(All neighbors are barbarians,
that goes without saying,
though you too have a trashcan.)

We make too much noise,
you know nothing about us,
you would like us to move away.

Come to our backyard, we say,
friendly and envious,
but you don't come.

Instead you quarrel
among yourselves, discussing
genealogies and the mortgage,
while the smoke from our tireless barbecues
blackens the roses.

iv

The investigator is here,
proclaiming his own necessity.
He has come to clean your heart.

Is it pure white,
or is there blood in it?

Stop this heart!
Cut this word from his mouth.
Cut this mouth.

    (Expurgation: purge.
    To purge is to clean,
    also to kill.)

For so much time, our history
was written in bones only.

Our flag has been silence,
which was mistaken for no flag,
which was mistaken for peace.

v

Is this what we wanted,
this politics, our hearts
flattened and strung out
from the backs of helicopters?

We thought we were talking
about a certain light

through the window of an empty room,
a light beyond the wet black trunks
of trees in this leafless forest
just before spring,
a certain loss.

We wanted to describe the snow,
the snow here, at the corner
of the house and orchard
in a language so precise
and secret it was not even
a code, it was snow,
there could be no translation.

To save this language
we needed echoes,
we needed to push back
the other words, the coarse ones
spreading themselves everywhere
like thighs or starlings.

No forests of discarded
crusts and torn underwear for us.
We needed guards.

Our hearts are flags now,
they wave at the end of each
machine we can stick them on.
Anyone can understand them.

They inspire pride,
they inspire slogans and tunes
you can dance to, they are redder than ever.

vi

Despite us
there is only one universe, the sun

burns itself slowly out no matter
what you say, is that
so?   The man
up to his neck in whitehot desert
sand disagrees.

> Close your eyes now, see:
> red sun, black sun, ordinary
> sun, sunshine, sun-
> king, sunlight soap, the sun
> is an egg, a lemon, a pale eye,
> a lion, sun
> on the beach, ice on the sun.

Language, like the mouths
that hold and release
it, is wet & living, each

word is wrinkled
with age, swollen
with other words, with blood, smoothed by
    the numberless
flesh tongues that have passed across it.

Your language hangs around your neck,
a noose, a heavy necklace;
each word is empire,
each word is vampire and mother.

As for the sun, there are as many
suns as there are words for sun;

false or true?

vii

Our leader
is a man of water
with a tinfoil skin.

He has two voices,
therefore two heads, four eyes,
two sets of genitals, eight
arms and legs and forty
toes and fingers.
Our leader is a spider,

he traps words.
They shrivel in his mouth,
he leaves the skins.

Most leaders speak
for themselves, then
for the people.

Who does our leader speak for?
How can you use two languages
and mean what you say in both?

No wonder our leader scuttles
sideways, melts in hot weather,
corrodes in the sea, reflects
light like a mirror,
splits our faces, our wishes,
is bitter.

Our leader is a monster
sewn from dead soldiers,
a siamese twin.

Why should we complain?
He is ours and us,
we made him.

viii

If I were a foreigner, as you say,
instead of your second head,
you would be more polite.

Foreigners are not there:
they pass and repass through the air
like angels, invisible
except for their cameras, and the rustle
of their strange fragrance

but we are not foreigners
to each other; we are the pressure
on the inside of the skull, the struggle
among the rocks for more room,
the shove and giveway, the grudging love,
the old hatreds.

Why fear the knife
that could sever us, unless
it would cut not skin but brain?

ix

You can't live here without breathing
someone else's air,
air that has been used to shape
these hidden words that are not yours.

This word was shut
in the mouth of a small man
choked off by the rope and gold/
red drumroll

This word was deported

This word was guttural,
buried wrapped in a leather throat
wrapped in a wolfskin

This word lies
at the bottom of a lake
with a coral bead and a kettle

This word was scrawny,
denied itself from year
to year, ate potatoes,
got drunk when possible

This word died of bad water.

Nothing stays under
forever, everyone
wants to fly, whose language
is this anyway?

You want the air
but not the words that come with it:
breathe at your peril.

These words are yours,
though you never said them,
you never heard them, history
breeds death but if you kill
it you kill yourself.

What is a traitor?

x

This is the secret: these hearts
we held out to you, these party
hearts (our hands
sticky with adjectives
and vague love, our smiles
expanding like balloons)

, these candy hearts we sent you
in the mail, a whole
bouquet of hearts, large as a country,

these hearts, like yours,
hold snipers.

A tiny sniper, one in each heart,
curled like a maggot, pallid
homunculus, pinhead, glass-eyed fanatic,
waiting to be given life.

Soon the snipers will bloom
in the summer trees, they will eat
their needle holes through your windows

(Smoke and broken leaves, up close
what a mess, wet red glass
in the zinnia border,
Don't let it come to this, we said
before it did.)

Meanwhile, we refuse
to believe the secrets of our hearts,
these hearts of neat velvet,
moral as fortune cookies.

Our hearts are virtuous, they swell
like stomachs at a wedding,
plump with goodwill.

In the evenings the news seeps in
from foreign countries,
those places with unsafe water.
We listen to the war, the wars,
any old war.

xi

Surely in your language
no one can sing, he said, one hand
in the small-change pocket.

That is a language for ordering
the slaughter and gutting of hogs, for
counting stacks of cans. Groceries
are all you are good for. Leave
the soul to us. Eat shit.

In these cages, barred crates,
feet nailed to the floor, soft
funnel down the throat,
we are forced with nouns, nouns,
till our tongues are sullen and rubbery.
We see this language always
and merely as a disease
of the mouth. Also
as the hospital that will cure us,
distasteful but necessary.

These words slow us, stumble
in us, numb us, who
can say even Open
the door, without these diffident
smiles, apologies?

Our dreams though
are of freedom, a hunger
for verbs, a song
which rises liquid and effortless,
our double, gliding beside us
over all these rivers, borders,
over ice or clouds.

Our other dream: to be mute.

Dreams are not bargains,
they settle nothing.

This is not a debate
but a duet
with two deaf singers.

THE BUS TO ALLISTON, ONTARIO

Snow packs the roadsides, sends dunes
onto the pavement, moves
through vision like a wave or sandstorm.
The bus charges this winter,
a whale or blunt gray
tank, wind whipping its flank.

Inside, we sit wool-
swathed and over-furred, made stodgy
by the heat, our boots
puddling the floor, our Christmas bundles
stuffed around us in the seats, the paper bags
already bursting; we trust

the driver, who is plump and garrulous, familiar
as a neighbor, which he is
to the thirty souls he carries, as
carefully as the time-
table permits; he knows
by experience the fragility of skulls.

Travel is dangerous; nevertheless, we travel.
The talk, as usual,
is of disasters: trainwrecks, fires,
herds of cattle killed in floods,
the malice of weather and tractors,
the clogging of hearts known
and unknown to us, illness and death,
true cases of buses

such as ours,
which skid, which hurtle
through snake fences and explode
with no survivors.
The woman talking says she heard
their voices at the crossroad
one night last fall, and not
a drop taken.

The dead ride with us on this bus,
whether we like it or not,
discussing aunts and suicides,
wars and the price of wheat,
fogging the close air, hugging us,
repeating their own deaths through these mouths,
cramped histories, violent
or sad, earthstained, defeated, proud,
the pain in small print, like almanacs,
mundane as knitting.

In the darkness, each distant house
glows and marks time,
is as true in attics
and cellars as in its steaming rich
crackling and butter kitchens.
The former owners, coupled and multiple,
seep through the mottled plaster, sigh
along the stairs they once rubbed concave
with their stiff boots, still envious,
breathe roasts and puddings through the floors;

it's wise
to set an extra plate.
How else can you live but with the knowledge
of old lives continuing in fading
sepia blood under your feet?

Outside, the moon is fossil
white, the sky cold purple, the stars
steely and hard; when there are trees they are dried
coral; the snow
is an unbroken spacelit
desert through which we make
our ordinary voyage,
those who hear voices and those
who do not, moving together, warm
and for the moment safe,
along the invisible road towards home.

NASTURTIUM

·

Nasturtium, with all its colors
from old moon to cut vein,
flower of deprivation,
does best in poor soil,
can be eaten, adds
blood to the salad.

I can choose to enter
this room, or not to enter.
Outside, pile of sand,
pile of stones, thistles
pushing between them, cement
blocks, two discarded mattresses,
mounds of red clay.

The dead stand in the wheatfield,
unseen by all but one girl;
her clothing blows in the east wind,
theirs does not.

Inside, there is nothing
to speak of: a table, a chair.
The room does nothing,
but like a cave it magnifies.

The woman up the road
foretells the weather
from signs known only to her,
before an accident

can smell blood on the stairs.
Should this be cured?

On the floor, caked mud, ashes
left from the winter.
Matches, a candle
in a holder shaped like a fish.

This is the room where I live
most truly, or cease to live.

Nasturtium is the flower
of prophecy; or not,
as you choose.

SOLSTICE POEM

i

A tree hulks in the living-
room, prickly monster, our hostage
from the wilderness, prelude
to light in this dark space of the year
which turns again toward the sun
today, or at least we hope so.

Outside, a dead tree
swarming with blue and yellow
birds; inside, a living one
that shimmers with hollow silver
planets and wafer faces,
salt and flour, with pearl
teeth, tin angels, a knitted bear.

This is our altar.

ii

Beyond the white hill which maroons us,
out of sight of the white
eye of the pond, geography

is crumbling, the nation
splits like an iceberg, factions
shouting Good riddance from the floes
as they all melt south,

with politics the usual
rats' breakfast.

All politicians are amateurs:
wars bloom in their heads like flowers
on wallpaper, pins strut on their maps.
Power is wine with lunch
and the right pinstripes.

There are no amateur soldiers.
The soldiers grease their holsters,
strap on everything
they need to strap, gobble their dinners.
They travel quickly and light.

The fighting will be local,
they know, and lethal.
Their eyes flick from target
to target: window, belly, child.
The goal is not to get killed.

iii

As for the women, who did not
want to be involved, they are involved.

It's that blood on the snow
which turns out to be not
some bludgeoned or machine-gunned
animal's, but your own
that does it.

Each has a knitting needle
stuck in her abdomen, a red pincushion
heart complete with pins,
a numbed body
with one more entrance than the world finds safe,
and not much money.

Each fears her children sprout
from the killed children of others.
Each is right.

Each has a father.
Each has a mad mother
and a necklace of lightblue tears.
Each has a mirror
which when asked replies Not you.

iv

My daughter crackles paper, blows
on the tree to make it live, festoons
herself with silver.
So far she has no use
for gifts.

What can I give her,
what armor, invincible
sword or magic trick, when that year comes?

How can I teach her
some way of being human
that won't destroy her?

I would like to tell her, Love
is enough, I would like to say,
Find shelter in another skin.

I would like to say, Dance
and be happy. Instead I will say
in my crone's voice, Be
ruthless when you have to, tell
the truth when you can,
when you can see it.

Iron talismans, and ugly, but
more loyal than mirrors.

v

In this house (in a dying orchard,
behind it a tributary
of the wilderness, in front a road),
my daughter dances
unsteadily with a knitted bear.

Her father, onetime soldier,
touches my arm.
Worn language clots our throats,
making it difficult to say
what we mean, making it
difficult to see.

Instead we sing in the back room, raising
our pagan altar
of oranges and silver flowers:
our fools' picnic, our signal,
our flame, our nest, our fragile golden
protest against murder.

Outside, the cries of the birds
are rumors we hear clearly
but can't yet understand. Fresh ice
glints on the branches.
                    In this dark
space of the year, the earth
turns again toward the sun, or

we would like to hope so.

THE WOMAN MAKES PEACE
WITH HER FAULTY HEART

•

It wasn't your crippled rhythm
I could not forgive, or your dark red
skinless head of a vulture

but the things you hid:
five words and my lost
gold ring, the fine blue cup
you said was broken,
that stack of faces, gray
and folded, you claimed
we'd both forgotten,
the other hearts you ate,
and all that discarded time you hid
from me, saying it never happened.

There was that, and the way
you would not be captured,
sly featherless bird, fat raptor
singing your raucous punctured song
with your talons and your greedy eye
lurking high in the molten sunset
sky behind my left cloth breast
to pounce on strangers.

How many times have I told you:
The civilized world is a zoo,
not a jungle, stay in your cage.
And then the shouts
of blood, the rage as you threw yourself
against my ribs.

As for me, I would have strangled you
gladly with both hands,
squeezed you closed, also
your yelps of joy.
Life goes more smoothly without a heart,
without that shiftless emblem,
that flyblown lion, magpie, cannibal
eagle, scorpion with its metallic tricks
of hate, that vulgar magic,
that organ the size and color
of a scalded rat,
that singed phoenix.

But you've shoved me this far,
old pump, and we're hooked
together like conspirators, which
we are, and just as distrustful.
We know that, barring accidents,
one of us will finally
betray the other; when that happens,
it's me for the urn, you for the jar.
Until then, it's an uneasy truce,
and honor between criminals.

MARSH, HAWK

Diseased or unwanted
trees, cut into pieces, thrown
away here, damp and soft in the sun, rotting and half-
covered with sand, burst truck
tires, abandoned, bottles and cans hit
with rocks or bullets, a mass grave,
someone made it, spreads on the
land like a bruise and we stand on it, vantage
point, looking out over the marsh.

Expanse of green
reeds, patches of water, shapes
just out of reach of the eyes,
the wind moves, moves it and it
eludes us, it is full
daylight. From the places
we can't see, the guttural swamp voices
impenetrable, not human,
utter their one-note
syllables, boring and
significant as oracles and quickly over.

It will not answer, it will not
answer, though we hit
it with rocks, there is a splash, the wind
covers it over; but
intrusion is not what we want,

we want it to open, the marsh rushes
to bend aside, the water
to accept us, it is only
revelation, simple as the hawk
which lifts up now against
the sun and into
our eyes, wingspread and sharp call
filling the head/sky, this,

to immerse, to have it slide
through us, disappearance
of the skin, this is what we are looking for,
the way in.

DAYBOOKS II

8

BLACK STONE MOTHER GOD

I chose from a lake's
edge, rests on the table
where I put her:
inert, all power
circled between thumb and finger.

From one side, an eye,
a head, a breast, a buttock.
From the other
a black potato,
a knob of earth, a long plum, a plump
elbow. A river shaped her,
smoothed her with sand and battered
her against the shore, and she
resisted, she is still here.

Worship what
you like, what you want
to be like . Old mother,
I pray to what is
and what refuses.

9

You wanted to give me something:
a cactus. You said

*I looked for one with flowers
but there weren't any.*

The cactus sat in its pot
of sand & stones, round
as a paperweight.
It did not grow or flower.

It could not be touched
without pain; finally

it could not be touched.

What was it you wanted
to say or offer?

Something different from what I have,
this clenched green apple, small

knowledge, thorny heart, this fist
shut against the desert air

(which however still guards
its one mouthful of water)

10

Every summer the apples
condense out of nothing
on their stems in the wet air
like sluggish dewdrops
or the tree bleeding.

Every fall they fall
and are eaten,
by us or something else,
wasps or snails, beetles,
the sandpaper mouths of the earth.

Every winter a few remain
on the branches, pulpy & brown,
wrinkled as kidneys or midget brains,
the only flesh in sight.

In spring we say the word *apple*
but it means nothing;
we can't remember those flavors,
we are blunt & thankless

But the apples condense again
out of nothing on their stems
like the tree bleeding; something
has this compassion.

11

APPLE JELLY

No sense in all this picking,
peeling & simmering
if sheer food is all
you want; you can buy it cheaper.

Why then do we burn our hours
& muscles in this stove,
cut our thumbs, to get these tiny
glass pots of clear jelly?

Hoarded in winter: the sun
on that noon, your awkward leap
down from the tree,
licked fingers, sweet pink juice,
what we keep
the taste of the act, taste
of this day.

12

How you disappear
in time, how you
disappear;

Who notices air?

Who could stand
a life all foreground?

Some days, yes, you fill
all the windows; some days you are
feverish and heavy, your bones
glow through the skin,
in winter even your shadow's
an ember on the floor;

But mostly this spring
you disappear
gradually into the sparse fringe
of willows on the other side
of the smoky pond,

into the dogwood; the melting snow
smudges your footprints

into
the not quite green

you disappear

Who notices air
except when it is gone.

13

APRIL, RADIO, PLANTING, EASTER

In the air-
waves, on the contrary,
there is a lot of noise
but no good news

and there's a limit to how much
you can take of this battering
against the ears without imploding
like some land animal drifting down
into the blackout of ocean, its body
an eye crushed by pliers

so you fashion yourself a helmet
of thickened skin
and move cautiously among the chairs
prepared for ambush,
impervious to the wiry screams
and toy pain of the others.

But there is one rift, one flaw:
that vulnerable bud, knot,

hole in the belly where you were nailed
to the earth forever.

I do not mean *the earth,* I mean the
earth that is here and browns your
feet, thickens your fingers,
unfurls in your brain and in
these onion seedlings
I set in flats lovingly under
a spare window.

We do not walk on the earth
but in it, wading
in that acid sea
where flesh is etched from
molten bone and re-forms.

In this massive tide
warm as liquid
sun, all waves are one
wave; there is no *other.*

LIGHTNING

Lightning slithers along the line
of the far hill:
a thousand and two, then thunder.

The air seeping up
from the half-cellar thickens
with wood-rot and damp cement.

Dog lies outside in his mudhole.
My small daughter
smears blue paint on the floor;
she smells of rancid butter.
The grass breathes fog.

Thunder, something is breaking,
a thousand and one, in the sky
right overhead, the ceiling

is leaking, the lights
go off, we laugh and are safe.

But there is also
the dry sound of rain on the pond,
feather against the ear, silence.

This is not thunder, this is the future.
A thousand and four, a thousand and five,
my heartbeat recedes down the driveway,

moving along the row of maples
like slow footsteps, and stops

where I wait for both of us,
dark moon in an unmarked calendar,
a silhouette, an absence.

THE PUPPET OF THE WOLF

i

The puppet of the wolf
I have not made yet
encloses my right hand:
fur stubbles my wrists,
a tongue, avid, carnivorous,
licks between thumb and finger;
my knuckles bunch into eyes,
eyes of opaque flesh,
cunning but sightless.

The wolf is transparent, but visible:
my daughter sees it,
my right hand is the wolf.
She laughs at its comic
dance, at its roars
and piglet murders:
the bones of my left hand
squeak and crack in its grip,
in its gray teeth,
its lack of mercy.

The last house crashes down:
the wolf is on fire,
my right hand is on fire,
the wolf is gone.

ii

Where has the wolf gone?
He disappeared
under the skin of my fingers,
my scalded werewolf hand,
which now, restored to normal,
slides like an ordinary
hand past the seahorse
and orange boat of the bath.

This is a miracle, there is never
any death:
the wolf comes back whenever
he is called,
unwounded and intact;
piglets jump from my thumbs.

My dying right
hand, which knots and shrinks
drier and more cynical
each year, is immortal,
briefly, and innocent.

Together with my left hand, its
enemy and prey, it chases
my daughter through the warm air,
and muted with soapsuds, lifts her
into the water.

A RED SHIRT

(For Ruth)

i

My sister and I are sewing
a red shirt for my daughter.
She pins, I hem, we pass the scissors
back & forth across the table.

Children should not wear red,
a man once told me.
Young girls should not wear red.

In some countries it is the color
of death; in others passion,
in others war, in others anger,
in others the sacrifice

of shed blood. A girl should be
a veil, a white shadow, bloodless
as a moon on water; not
dangerous; she should

keep silent and avoid
red shoes, red stockings, dancing.
Dancing in red shoes will kill you.

ii

But red is our color by birth-

right, the color of tense joy
& spilled pain that joins us

to each other. We stoop over
the table, the constant pull

of the earth's gravity furrowing
our bodies, tugging us down.

The shirt we make is stained
with our words, our stories.

The shadows the light casts
on the wall behind us multiply:

This is the procession
of old leathery mothers,

the moon's last quarter
before the blank night,

mothers like worn gloves
wrinkled to the shapes of their lives,

passing the work from hand to hand,
mother to daughter,

a long thread of red blood, not yet broken.

iii

Let me tell you the story
about the Old Woman.

First: she weaves your body.
Second: she weaves your soul.

Third: she is hated & feared,
though not by those who know her.

She is the witch you burned
by daylight and crept from your home

to consult & bribe at night. The love
that tortured you you blamed on her.

She can change her form,
and like your mother she is covered with fur.

The black Madonna
studded with miniature

arms & legs, like tin stars,
to whom they offer agony

and red candles when there is no other
help or comfort, is also her.

iv

It is January, it's raining, this gray
ordinary day. My
daughter, I would like
your shirt to be just a shirt,
no charms or fables. But fables
and charms swarm here
in this January world,
entrenching us like snow, and few
are friendly to you; though
they are strong,
potent as viruses
or virginal angels dancing
on the heads of pins,
potent as the hearts
of whores torn out
by the roots because they were thought
to be solid gold, or heavy
as the imaginary
jewels they used to split
the heads of Jews for.

It may not be true
that one myth cancels another.
Nevertheless, in a corner
of the hem, where it will not be seen,
where you will inherit
it, I make this tiny
stitch, my private magic.

V

The shirt is finished: red
with purple flowers and pearl
buttons. My daughter puts it on,

hugging the color
which means nothing to her
except that it is warm
and bright. In her bare

feet she runs across the floor,
escaping from us, her new game,
waving her red arms

in delight, and the air
explodes with banners.

NIGHT POEM

.

There is nothing to be afraid of,
it is only the wind
changing to the east, it is only
your father   the thunder
your mother   the rain

In this country of water
with its beige moon damp as a mushroom,
its drowned stumps and long birds
that swim, where the moss grows
on all sides of the trees
and your shadow is not your shadow
but your reflection,

your true parents disappear
when the curtain covers your door.
We are the others,
the ones from under the lake
who stand silently beside your bed
with our heads of darkness.
We have come to cover you
with red wool,
with our tears and distant whispers.

You rock in the rain's arms,
the chilly ark of your sleep,
while we wait, your night
father and mother,
with our cold hands and dead flashlight,
knowing we are only
the wavering shadows thrown
by one candle, in this echo
you will hear twenty years later.

ALL BREAD

All bread is made of wood,
cow dung, packed brown moss,
the bodies of dead animals, the teeth
and backbones, what is left
after the ravens. This dirt
flows through the stems into the grain,
into the arm, nine strokes
of the axe, skin from a tree,
good water which is the first
gift, four hours.

Live burial under a moist cloth,
a silver dish, the row
of white famine bellies
swollen and taut in the oven,
lungfuls of warm breath stopped
in the heat from an old sun.

Good bread has the salt taste
of your hands after nine
strokes of the axe, the salt
taste of your mouth, it smells
of its own small death, of the deaths
before and after.

Lift these ashes
into your mouth, your blood;
to know what you devour
is to consecrate it,
almost. All bread must be broken
so it can be shared. Together
we eat this earth.

YOU BEGIN

You begin this way:
this is your hand,
this is your eye,
that is a fish, blue and flat
on the paper, almost
the shape of an eye.
This is your mouth, this is an O
or a moon, whichever
you like. This is yellow.

Outside the window
is the rain, green
because it is summer, and beyond that
the trees and then the world,
which is round and has only
the colors of these nine crayons.

This is the world, which is fuller
and more difficult to learn than I have said.
You are right to smudge it that way

with the red and then
the orange: the world burns.

Once you have learned these words
you will learn that there are more
words than you can ever learn.
The word *hand* floats above your hand
like a small cloud over a lake.
The word *hand* anchors
your hand to this table,
your hand is a warm stone
I hold between two words.

This is your hand, these are my hands, this is the world,
which is round but not flat and has more colors
than we can see.

It begins, it has an end,
this is what you will
come back to, this is your hand.

NOTES

•

MARRYING THE HANGMAN

Jean Cololère, a drummer in the colonial troops at Québec, was imprisoned for duelling in 1751. In the cell next to his was Françoise Laurent, who had been sentenced to hang for stealing. Except for letters of pardon, the only way at the time for someone under sentence of death to escape hanging was, for a man, to become a hangman, or, for a woman, to marry one. Françoise persuaded Cololère to apply for the vacant (and undesirable) post of executioner, and also to marry her.

> —Condensed from the *Dictionary of Canadian Biography*, Volume III, 1741-1770*

* My thanks to Howard Engel for drawing this entry to my attention.

After the failure of the uprising in Lower Canada (now Québec) in 1838, the British army and an assortment of volunteers carried out reprisals against the civilian population around Beauharnois, burning houses and barns and turning the inhabitants out into the snow. No one was allowed to give them shelter and many froze to death. The men were arrested as rebels; those who were not home were presumed to be rebels and their houses were burned.

The volunteers from Glengarry were Scots, most of them in Canada because their houses had also been burned during the Highland Clearances, an aftermath of the British victory at Culloden.

Dufferin, Simcoe, and Grey are the names of three counties in Ontario, settled around this period.

(continued from copyright page)

Parnassus, Field, Open Places, The Nation, MS Magazine (U.S.)

Helix, Mewanjin (Australia)

Some have been broadcast on the CBC and some on the BBC.

ABOUT THE AUTHOR

Margaret Atwood is the author of four novels—*The Edible Woman, Surfacing, Lady Oracle,* and most recently the highly praised *Life Before Man*—as well as eight books of poetry. Her writing has been acclaimed by critics in the United States, Canada, England and Europe.

Ms. Atwood lives on a farm near Alliston, Ontario, with novelist Graeme Gibson and their three-year-old daughter, Jess.